Finding
H.E.R.

Finding
H.E.R.

Marie Frazier

XULON PRESS ELITE

Xulon Press Elite
2301 Lucien Way #415
Maitland, FL 32751
407.339.4217
www.xulonpress.com

© 2021 by Marie Frazier

All rights reserved solely by the author. The author guarantees all contents are original and do not infringe upon the legal rights of any other person or work. No part of this book may be reproduced in any form without the permission of the author. The views expressed in this book are not necessarily those of the publisher.

Due to the changing nature of the Internet, if there are any web addresses, links, or URLs included in this manuscript, these may have been altered and may no longer be accessible. The views and opinions shared in this book belong solely to the author and do not necessarily reflect those of the publisher. The publisher, therefore, disclaims responsibility for the views or opinions expressed within the work.

Unless otherwise indicated, Scripture quotations taken from the Holy Bible, New International Version (NIV). Copyright © 1973, 1978, 1984, 2011 by Biblica, Inc.™. Used by permission. All rights reserved.

Paperback ISBN-13: 978-1-66282-484-5
Ebook ISBN-13: 978-1-66282-485-2

Introduction

Have you ever heard someone say, "It's her"? You know, in that tone of disapproval or disappointment? I have. I have heard that phrase my entire life for as long as I can remember, and each time I've heard it has been just as gut-wrenching as the last. *Her.* For years, I felt like that pretty much summed up who I was—just her, not the popular girl, not the life of the party, not someone you had been missing or loved having around. Just her. Have you ever felt that way? Do you hear that phrase a lot? Do you feel like you have no other purpose in life but to be the expected disappointment in other people's circle? Well, if so, I am so glad you picked up this book and so glad that we are going to take this journey into her! Into you and the amazing woman God has created you to be!

So, buckle up, sister (I'm going to use this phrase a lot on our journey!), because you are not going to want to miss a single thing. Here is to becoming, embracing, being, and loving her!

Chapter One

When I was young (like super young but old enough to remember now that I am older), I was always referred to as the troublemaker. My younger sister (let's call her Winnie) and I were shipped back and forth from Florida to Georgia more times than I can count between the ages of four and fifteen. My dad had me at a young age of eighteen, and just like that, eleven months later, my sister was here. I know he didn't waste no time! My biological mom wasn't as interested in being a mom as much as she was drinking, so my dad shipped us off to his mom in Georgia. He got this itch to want to be a family every now and then, so we got to play *house* every time he thought he had found "mom" material in a woman.

Every time my dad got a new woman in his life, it was made known that my sister (the pretty one) was the good girl, and I was trouble. I never even had a chance when it came to meeting the probable stepmoms. I suppose that is where the looks of disappointment started in my life. I had a brown mess of tangled curly hair, a love for dirt and animals, and a voice that carried through the halls like a bullhorn.

My sister, however, was not one for dirt. She had beautiful straight brown hair and green doe eyes, the cutest laugh, and loved to cuddle on the couch with anyone willing to cuddle back. She was the pretty princess that (I thought) that most moms dream of when having little girls. She was a real-life Belle.

What I didn't realize, however, was that even though my sister was beautiful, there was beauty in the young girl I was back then too. It just looked different than the typical "princess" type.

From a young age, we are taught that perfection is in the cleanliness, bows, dresses, and smile of a young girl. We miss that there is beauty in strength. The little girl who wants to hit a home run or take care of stray dogs or even build things out of Legos is just as beautiful as the little girl walking the runway of the towns little miss beauty pageant. As mothers, aunts, grandmothers, and friends, we have to remind our little girls that princesses are great and beautiful, but so are athletes, doctors, lawyers, architects, stay-at-home moms, and so many other women with passions for things that aren't always clean, prim, and proper.

What makes us beautiful is our diversity and the way we use the passions God has given us to the best of our abilities. We are all created differently, uniquely, and with gifts given to us by our Father. Some of us share similar gifts, traits, and qualities with others, but no one woman uses her gift like another, even if it looks the same to the world. We can see the differences in each other, and that is beauty.

So, if like me, you have been labeled the troublemaker, the non-desirable child, or felt like you were running competition with a sibling, then I encourage you to remember these words. Write them on your mirror or a Post-it note where you can see it every day.

Jeremiah 1:5 says, "Before I formed you in your mother's womb, I knew you." This means that the One who created you knew exactly what you would be like before your mother even carried you. He knew everything about you—your tangled hair, loud voice, love for dirt, and the list goes on. Think about it: the Creator of the universe and worlds that we haven't even discovered looked down and thought it needed one of you, tangled hair and all! God only made one of you, so be her no matter what, and be the best version of her that you can possibly be, no matter what that looks like to others.

So, truth time. If I am being completely honest, I am a huge fan of people— talking, hanging out, going to dinner parties, and all that jazz. One of my favorite things to do is entertain at my home. I love planning and throwing parties. I will make up any excuse to have something to celebrate. I feel sorry for my kids and grandkids because it is probably overwhelming for them at times, but I just want them to cherish every moment of life and live in it. Our lives are reduced to a dash when it's all over, and I want them to make the most of it.

However, if you ask people who know me, they will tell you that I am an extreme introvert. I never talk unless spoken to, and I have a mean face and look intimidating or like I am always mad. This could not be farther from the truth, though. To be honest, it hurts my heart that this is how I am perceived. I allow my fear of rejection to cause me to be an introvert. Plainly put, if you don't speak to me first, I will never speak to you for fear of the "the look."

Some of you know what I mean. That look people give you when you begin a conversation or compliment them out of nowhere. Yeah, that one. I hate that look. Why can't I just be nice and love the shoes you are wearing or think that you did an amazing job on your make-up and clothing ensemble? Why can't I ask why you like watermelon in your oatmeal and find out that you have been eating it this way since you were five because that's how your grandmother made it?

I love meeting new people, finding out what they are passionate about, and creating new relationships. But, I hate the look more. So, for twenty or more years, I have let my fear create an introvert out of me. I have let fear make me be someone that I look at and wish I was someone else. I have let fear allow me to see extroverted people and long to be one of them. Hello, I am her! I am that girl. I just hide her away because of fear. Do you do this too? Are you terrified of the look?

Let's stop that right now! If you get the look, just move on. I was told that you only meet ten truly rude people in your life. If you have just had an encounter like this recently, then you got this—only nine more to go! Seriously, though, sometimes you are just going to meet people who are not nice. But think of all the relationships you can make by not allowing fear to control who you truly are. If you are an introvert and you're reading this, then maybe when someone like me comes up and asks why you like coconut milk in your coffee, just make conversation. You never know when and where an amazing relationship will start.

I met a girl a few years ago through a mutual friend. She was referred to me for a job she needed done. I run my own customization business, and she was looking to get some shirts made. I can't tell you how because I honestly do not have a clue, but this girl is like family now. We talk every single day. We encourage each other, pray together, and do life together, all because she was referred to me for a job. So, have the conversations, ask the crazy questions, and make the random compliments. In 1 Thessalonians 5:11, the Word says,

"Therefore encourage one another and build each other up just as in fact you are doing."

It's okay if some people give you the look. It's okay if some people don't want to get to know you. They are missing out, sis, and imagine all the people who will want to get to know you. Imagine what we are missing out on by not having the courage to just say hi occasionally. So, I challenge you to go out today and make a new acquaintance and see what happens. Let's build each other up and stop tearing each other down. We can do so much together.

Chapter Two

Guilt. I know, I know—believe me, no one wants to hear that word, much less see it or talk about it. Well, buckle up, sis, cause this chapter is gonna get bumpy. For the longest time, I believed that I was meant to live a life of pain. Didn't matter what kind. I made a choice as a ten-year-old girl that forever changed my life. My dad got married when I was nine years old. He swore he had found the perfect woman. She *was,* by all accounts, amazing—well, at least on the outside. She was so beautiful that I thought for sure she had to be a model. Her voice was super sweet, and she appeared to be gentle and kind. But behind closed doors, the sweetness melted, and all that was left was the most hateful, bitter, angry woman I have ever met in my entire life.

Now, sis, I have met my share of monsters disguised as people in my life. By the time I was five years old, I had been molested by a close relative, sold for drugs by my biological mom, and abandoned more times than I can count. So, when I tell you that this woman (let's call her "the wife") was the scariest monster I had ever encountered in my life, I *mean* it. After she and my dad got married, everything changed.

She became bitter and angry all the time. She started to become agitated at the smallest things and gained almost a hundred pounds. Now, I am not body shaming, but sometimes weight gain is due to a mental illness like depression. I don't know if that's what it was, but something was going on. The sweet lady we had met was not the woman who was now our stepmother. It was like it brought her joy to beat my sister and me. She would come up with new ways of inflicting pain and then test them like she was experimenting with the pain threshold of a child's body.

The beatings weren't enough at some point, so torture became her thrill, I guess. She found all kinds of things to inflict pain—boards, hot coffee, hot glue guns, bowling balls, and her favorite for a time, water boarding. If you don't know what water boarding is, I would say you're lucky. For an eleven-year-old girl, it was one of the scariest things I had ever experienced. It is like being drowned but you can only wish death would come to stop the fear that you feel.

I still look in the mirror at the scars that will never go away from her "experiments" on my body. I can still feel the heat from the cigarettes she put out on our faces and taste the blood that would fill my mouth every time her ring with fifteen diamonds in it hit my teeth. I can still feel the pain in my stomach from going days without eating. I can still hear my sister's screams when I close my eyes. I don't know if these things will ever go away.

Now, by the time I was ten, I knew to stay clear of her and just do what was expected of me. However, one day while cleaning, I picked up some papers that were folded together. I saw my dad's handwriting on them, so I wanted to read them. They were letters between him and his wife. Now, at this time, I would read anything and everything that I could get my hands on, so maybe some part of me read them because of that, and maybe the other part of me was curious at ten years old. I couldn't tell you for sure. After I finished reading them, I placed them in a file tray on the counter and went about cleaning, but this was not where I had found them.

A few hours later, I heard the wife calling for me and my sister. You know that sinking feeling you get when you know something bad is about to happen? Like, your heart has gone to your stomach, but you can't get it to go back to where it belongs, so it just sits there, heavy and uncomfortable? You want to throw up, but you know you can't, so the heaviness just gets worse and worse. Yeah. That is what I felt every single time she called my name.

We made our way into the kitchen where she was holding the letters in her hand. She was fuming. Her face had to be as red as a fire truck. She asked who had moved the letters. I told her I had. I explained that I had found them and moved them while cleaning. Are you sitting down, sis? This is where the journey takes an immediate detour.

She then asked if either one of us had read the letters. We both quickly replied no. I know what you're thinking—kids lie all the time. No biggie, right? Wrong! The wife then pulled out a Bible. She looked at both of us and said that if we were telling the truth, to lay our hands on the Bible and swear to God that Satan could have our souls if we were lying. Are you still sitting down?

My sister, of course, did it with no hesitation because she knew she hadn't read them. As I watched her do this, I thought to myself, *If I admit it now, she is going to split my face open or worse. I'm young, and this probably won't even count, right?*

God will understand, right? So, I laid my hand on the Bible and said those words.

Now, if she ever picks up this book and reads it, this will be the moment when she knows that I read the letters thirty years later. Guess what? It has taken me almost that long to let this incident go. Yes, sis, thirty years. I believed from that moment on that God had cursed me and my life because I had told that lie to escape a beating.

No matter how many people have told me that God is not a God of condemnation. No matter how many people have told me that God forgives and forgets.

No matter how many people have told me that God doesn't hold it against me.

I was meant to live in pain because ten-year-old me made a choice. I was abused, molested, raped, beaten, cheated on, betrayed, and medically cursed because I didn't want to endure another beating at ten years old. There was no way God could love me after I swore on His Word and said those awful words.

I wish sometimes I could go back and hug that little girl and tell her that God loves her no matter what. I wish I could tell her that people make mistakes every day and God still loves them. I wish I could share the story of Peter with her when he denied Jesus but God still used him to build His church. But I can't. It doesn't work that way, and how would I be able to share this with you if I could?

I am here today full of God's love, mercy, grace, and acceptance to tell you that our God is *not* a God of condemnation. Nothing on this earth will separate you from His love. He promised us this in His Word. Romans 8:38-39 says,

"For I am convinced that neither death nor life, neither angels nor demons, neither the present nor the future nor any powers neither height nor depth nor anything else in all creation will be able to separate us from the love of God that is in Christ Jesus."

Did you get that, sis? "Nor anything in all creation"! Not even a scared ten-year old's crazy idea to swear on the Bible and lie. Now, don't hear what

I'm not saying. What I did was wrong. I am not condoning lying on the Word of God. But God is not cursing, shunning, or condemning me for this mistake. He sent Jesus for this very reason. We are humans, and we make mistakes, sometimes colossal ones. That is why the verse states that we have this *in* Christ Jesus.

Sometimes we need a lifeline, and God gave us one in Jesus. So, I don't know what you've done. I don't know if you were a scared little girl like me or maybe you are a scared young woman. Either way, God loves you, sis. He loves you so much that He sent His Son to take on that crazy mistake that you feel like you will never be able to forget or be forgiven for. Maybe you are so sure that your deed is unforgivable that you haven't even asked for forgiveness. Sis, the Father is waiting. Go to Him. He doesn't desire nor take pleasure in your pain. Sometimes He allows the pain, but He will always see you through it.

Think about this. What if your child was an addict and stole $5,000 from you and ran away.

However, three years later, they got clean and turned their life around but didn't reach out to you because they carried the guilt of what they had done. Wouldn't you want them to come to you? Wouldn't you forgive them? Would you want them to carry that guilt forever? Of course not.

God doesn't want you to either. He wants you to come to Him. He longs for relationship with you. That is what we were created for. All it takes is one step, sis. Just one. Don't let Satan convince you that God wants you to live in pain or guilt. He did that to me for almost thirty years. I don't know what year you're on, but make it the last one now. The Father is waiting. He always was.

Chapter Three

Betrayal. Yeah, sis, we gotta talk about it. I know, I know—we just covered a tough subject. We just gotta dive in sometimes, even when it's heavy. However, the beauty of books is that if you need a minute to breathe or to step away for a day to talk to Jesus, then you can do that. Just go at your own pace. These words aren't going anywhere, and God knows when you and your heart are ready for them.

Betrayal is something I have been on the receiving end of much more than I would like to admit by people I never thought would hurt me this way. I know we have all heard that a million times, but we still let our hearts trust and wish for the best. We want to see the good in people even when sometimes it just isn't there. I've been down a dark path that I'm going to share for the first time ever.

It is a different kind of pain when someone betrays you. It's not only your heart that hurts. It's your mind, spirit, and sometimes even your body. I've been there. It's like the weight of a semi-truck has landed on you, and all you can do is wave your arms and struggle to breathe. It is like you stop completely, and all you can do is watch the world move around you. Sometimes you can move with the world and just go through the motions of your day and pray that something will take you out of this black hole because you don't have the courage to do it yourself. Yes, sis, it is about to get very real, raw, emotional, and dark for a minute. Buckle up.

I've been married to the same man for twenty years this year. He is amazing. He has supported every crazy idea I have ever had, no matter how much the cost or loss. He has stood beside me through every surgery, health phenomenon, dark day, and tear. I could not have asked God for a better partner in life. But...yep, you guessed it—there is always a but, right. Things have not always been roses and sunshine. He betrayed me. Yes, this amazing, loving, devoted husband betrayed me.

We moved to Florida to start over in 2009 because we wanted better for our two boys and our family. My half-sister (let's call her Jane) already lived in Florida. She was the only child from my dad's marriage to the woman we talked about in the last chapter. Jane was my best friend in the whole world—not just because she was my sister but because we had more in common than anyone on the planet. There is not a single memory from 2012 back that does not have her in it. We were inseparable. So, when we moved to Florida, Jane moved in.

Jane watched over my boys while my husband and I worked, and she was like a second mom to them. I loved the fact that while I was working, they had someone who loved them and would care for them the way I did. It helped me out tremendously when I became sick and started spending a lot of time in the hospital. Doctors could not figure out what was wrong with me. I was having blackouts and pain in my stomach. Even after three different surgeries, they were clueless, but that is a story for another day.

In 2011, Jane came by my job and said she wanted to talk. She informed me that she was pregnant as the result of a one-night stand. She seemed upset by the fact, but I was ecstatic. I was going on and on telling her how we had always dreamed and talked about raising our children together, how she was going to be a wonderful mother. I was beside myself with joy for her. She finally started smiling, and we began chatting about the new baby, names, and all the things that come with pregnancy. Life was perfect to me at this point. I had an amazing little family, and now my best friend was adding to hers. It was a blissful three weeks.

On the day of Jane's first sonogram, she called me at work. She told me that she had made a mistake and was eight weeks along rather than three. Now, don't ask me why, sis—I couldn't explain it if I tried, but my stomach started to turn, and the excitement I had felt for the last three weeks melted away in that moment. As soon as we hung up the phone, I went to my calendar. Tracing back eight to nine weeks, I realized something that made me sick. Jane had either gotten pregnant the week of my son's eighth birthday or the week of Fourth of July. She was with my family both weeks, and the only male in the group was my husband.

I immediately called my sister Winnie and asked her to talk me down, to tell me that I was being irrational. She did her best. She told me what anyone else would have said—that my husband loved me, that he would never do anything like this to me or our boys. I began to get physically sick. Not just nausea, I lost my voice and felt weak. I called and told my boss that I had to get home. So, I went home and went to bed. I told myself as I closed my eyes that this was a bad dream. When I opened my eyes, things would be perfect, just like they had been for the past ten years.

When I woke up, my husband was sitting on the bed next to me. He was wringing his hands, and his head was down. I could see pain in his face and his eyes when he looked up. I asked what was wrong as my heart started to drop into my stomach, and he dropped his head and uttered the words that no one ever wants to hear.

"We need to talk."

What it is about that phrase that literally makes people ill, I don't know, but it is absolutely volatile. I sat up and waited for him to speak. He didn't. I knew. In my heart, head, mind, and spirit, I knew. He said he needed to tell me something, but he didn't want to lose me. I hoarsely spoke and told him,

"I know. I know, but I want to hear you say it."

Now, truth be told, sis, I could have gone my whole life without hearing those words, but I asked for it, and I got it.

"I slept with Jane."

Remember what I said about when you just stop and the world continues around you? Yep, that was this moment. He cried, talked, waved his hands, and shook his head, and all I could do was just be. I don't know if I was breathing; I don't know if I was crying, screaming, or dying; I just don't know. It's like looking at the most beautiful stained-glass ceiling you have ever laid eyes on, and suddenly, it comes crashing down on you. You feel every cut, scrape, burn, and piece piercing your entire being.

How? Why? Did I do something to deserve this? Did I not live up to my vows? Was I not enough? Was I not the person he committed his life to? Had I changed? Did she have something I didn't? Were they in love? So many questions, but no answers.

The next day, we entered the going-through-the-motions phase I talked about. I drove my children to school. On the way there, my oldest son decided that he didn't feel good so he didn't want to go. I drove home and told him to go lay in his room. I sat on the couch and listened to my phone continue to vibrate. At this point, I had turned the ringer off. Jane had called anyone who would listen and told them what was going on. My phone did not stop ringing from that moment on.

"What are you going to do, Marie? What about the boys, Marie? Are you gonna stay with your husband, Marie? Are you still good with Jane, Marie? Will you love and accept Jane's baby, Marie? Will the baby call you Aunt or Mama Marie?" And on and on and on. I threw the phone on the floor and walked to my medicine cabinet.

My head was spinning, my eyes were burning, and my chest was caving in. I can remember the physical pain like it was yesterday. It was worse than any beating I ever took as a child. I couldn't fix it. I couldn't make it stop. I just wanted to close my eyes and when I opened them, realize I was having a nightmare. You know, the ones that seem so real you wake up and your face is wet against the pillow from crying in your sleep.

I stood there for a minute and watched the counter fill with tears. *They would be happy if I wasn't in the way,* I thought. *Jane has been like a mom to my boys, and now she and my husband are having a baby. I am the only piece that doesn't fit.* I pulled out every pill bottle I had been prescribed for pain and anxiety, dumped them on the counter, just started taking them. I just wanted everything to stop, but mostly the pain. Then I felt something on my back.

I turned around to see my eight-year-old son standing in front of me. Tears were running down my face, I had three more pills in my hand. I couldn't do anything but just stand there. He took my hand and said, "Mama, that is enough medicine," and led me to the couch and sat down. He gently pulled my head down on his lap and began rubbing my face and repeating, "It's gonna be okay, Mama. It's gonna be okay." All I could think in that moment was, I am an adult. *The mom. The protector. How is it that my eight-year-old has more strength right now than I do? I should be the one being strong for him!*

I fell apart in that eight-year old's lap.

Now, I know what some of you may be thinking. *How could she do that? Why would she try to kill herself when she had two kids? How could she let her son pick up her broken pieces? What kind of person let's a child pick up her broken pieces?*

Well, sis, I honestly only have one answer for you. I don't know. I love my boys more than life itself. Since before I can remember, the only thing I ever wanted to be was a mom. I would love to tell you that I held it together and was the person that my children looked to to get through this stage in life, but I wasn't. I would love to say I played some worship music and got it together. I would love to say I went to church and found the answer, but I can't do that because I promised to be honest. That means even when it's difficult and ugly.

I fell apart for months. I don't remember most of those days. I just went through the daily motions. I cried when people couldn't see me. I asked God why. I begged Him to take me from this world. I had nothing left to give to anyone and no possible way to fight anything else that life could throw at me. Then I got an answer. Some things in life, God gives us the strength for, and others, we need His strength for.

I couldn't and wouldn't be with my husband today if it were not for the strength and love of

God in me. There is no part of my human self that could forgive or love the man who betrayed me the way he did. It is all God. Not too long after this, my husband gave his life to Christ and completely changed. I would love to tell you that my relationship with Jane was restored, but unfortunately, I cannot. This was something that hurt me for many years until I realized that sometimes God removes people from your life because they can not go where He has called you. I have forgiven her and pray daily for the absolute best for her and her family.

People have and continue to ask me how I forgave them. Well, as bad as my betrayal story is, there is one that is harsher. Jesus was betrayed too. He was betrayed by the people closest to Him, yet He forgave them all, even dying on the cross to save them from themselves. I always ask, are we any better than Jesus? No. Jesus called us to forgive just as He forgave us.

Now, sis, don't hear what I'm not saying. Forgiveness isn't a pass to let people walk all over you.

There are people in the world who will abuse your forgiveness. You don't have to live with someone in your life to forgive them. My pastor says that forgiving doesn't mean forgetting. It means you can move on with your life without wishing ill will on the person who has hurt you. I don't wish bad things for Jane. I pray she is at peace with herself and that she prospers and has a good life. I don't hound my husband with questions, track his phone, or hold it over him about what he did. I want good for both of them.

My husband is not the man he was ten years ago. He is not the same. He is a new creation in Christ Jesus, and I see it every day in him and his life. He serves others, he has broken generational curses, and he has beaten addictions. He is a man of God. I always tell him that he is a modern-day David. David was called a man after God's own heart in the Bible, and David made his share of mistakes. Adultery, murder, and lust are just a few. But God knew David's heart, just as He has always known my husband's. Once they surrendered to God, these two men did and will go on to accomplish amazing things in His name for His kingdom. They are testimonies to what God can do with the broken.

Yes, sis, broken. We are all broken without Him. Even when we look perfect on the outside, we are pieces on the inside waiting for our Maker to make us whole. My heart was not the only thing broken in this betrayal. My spirit was broken, and I had to call on my Maker to make it whole again so that I was capable of love, trust, and happiness with the man God chose for me.

Sis, the pain sucks, I know, but sometimes your journey isn't about you or where you are going. Sometimes it is about who God wants to reach *through* you. I firmly believe my husband would not be where he is today if we had not gone through this trial. I don't think he would know love if I had not listened to God and followed what I knew He was telling me. I know this will sound crazy, but I would go through it again for him to be where God has him today.

Yes, sis, every tear, every pain, every sleepless night. I would do it again. This is what kingdom work looks like. This is loving people where they are, despite what they have done. This is what Christ has called us to do. Now, I am not saying to lay down and let your spouse get away with adultery. That is not what happened here. With forgiveness came change. It is the same when we come to Christ. We are changed as He changes us. My husband changed as he allowed God to take control of his life.

Walking in the path Christ has for us is not always traveling the world. It's not always feeding the poor or helping the sick. It's not always fuzzy, warm, safe, or in our strongest abilities. Sometimes it is right in front of us. Sometimes it is a place we never imagined we would be. Sometimes it is right there in your home.

Chapter Four

Let's switch gears for a bit. We have been digging deep into some things that I know are hard to face. Believe me, it has taken me years to get to the point in my life where I can look back and see that God was working in my life the whole time. It's hard to see Him sometimes and we feel like He has abandoned us to our own misery, but that could not be farther from the truth of His character. Remember, I said all I ever wanted to be was a mom. Well, looking from a parent's point of view has helped me so much.

When my oldest son was born, it was the happiest day of my life. The seven months in and out of the hospital didn't matter. I was holding the most precious gift God had ever given me. I can still remember and feel the joy from that day. Not too long before I had gotten pregnant with my son, I had experienced the loss of a miscarriage. It crushed me, even more because the doctor had told me that my body was not meant to carry babies. There are certain hormones that your body produces to carry a baby to full term, and mine did not have them.

What a freak thing, I thought. *Didn't God create a woman to carry and bear children? Wasn't that the purpose of His command to be fruitful and multiply? How could my body not be equipped to do exactly what He made it for?* I started to fall into a depression. Then I started to pray. I prayed harder than I ever had before. God knew my heart. He knew I wanted to be a mother. He heard my cry, and I became pregnant with my son.

My pregnancy wasn't easy. I had to take supplements, and I was in the hospital for most of my pregnancy and then had to be induced because my body had started to shut down. Thankfully, my son was delivered healthy. That was the longest nine months of my life. Looking back, I see that God was with me through it all. If I am being honest, I was closer to Him during those nine months than I had been in many years. Then it hit me.

Sometimes when things are going great, we put our relationship with God on the shelf. We don't feel like we need Him when the sun is shining. We never stop to think about the storms He may be keeping us from that surround us each day. We were created to have a relationship with God. We are His creation created for His delight. When we get so focused on the things of this world, I think God allows us to experience what life is like without Him in it, but that doesn't mean He isn't there or that He has left us.

Let me explain it like this. When your child is a teenager, they can begin to think they need you less than they did when they were a child. Now what if they begin to have problems at school—socially, academically, etc.? You didn't leave them, but if they never communicate with you about what is going on, they are left to deal with the problems on their own. That doesn't mean that you won't help them or that you are not always there for them.

God has promised us in His Word that He will never leave us or forsake us (Heb. 13:5). God is not One to break His promises. He seeks a relationship with us, however, one of my favorite hip hop artists says it like this—it's hard to answer prayers when no one's praying to You.

We get so caught up in our everyday lives that God takes a back seat to whatever else is going on. We were given free will on purpose. God doesn't want to take over you like a robot. He wants you to choose to love Him and want a relationship with Him, just like you want your child to do with you. He wants to be a part of your whole life, not just the times when you can't figure things out; to celebrate your joys *and* comfort your pains, not just one or the other.

Sis, I am guilty of it too. I get so caught up with work and being a mom and wife that I put my prayer and quiet time to the side. Sometimes before I know it, days have gone by, and I haven't talked with God. I have found that keeping a prayer journal is super helpful. I absolutely love going back and looking at past entries. It is an amazing way to recap how God has responded in my life. Sometimes I don't even realize it until I go back and read some of my past prayers. I encourage you to start one if you haven't, and if you have, consider re-reading some of your entries and see how God showed up when you weren't paying attention. It is amazing and really encouraging.

Chapter Five

When I was fifteen years old, I ran away from home for the first time. Now, I didn't run away because I was a rebellious teen or because my parents wouldn't let me see the boy I liked. As I mentioned earlier, my stepmom was extremely abusive. On this particular day, she was curling her hair, and for some reason, she decided that my punishment for not correctly cleaning the bathroom should be her curling iron on my arm for ten seconds.

I can still smell the scent it made as she laid that curling iron on my arm. After the burn began to blister, she grabbed a spiral brush and ran it across the blisters. As the blisters burst, some of the blood got on her, so she pushed me out of the door and told me to go wrap something around my arm to cover the wound before my dad came home. We always had to cover up the marks and bruises before Dad got home. By the age of ten, I was a pro at stage makeup.

I did as I was told and then headed out to the backyard to clean the pool filter. I stared at our back gate for what seemed like hours. All I could think about was if I could just get away from here, then I would be okay. I couldn't leave my sister though. I had been trying for weeks to make her see that if we didn't leave, we were going to die, but she was too terrified. She thought that if we got caught, we would be killed, but I couldn't take it anymore. The more my arm started to sting, the more I felt the need to run. So, I did.

I lifted the latch and took off. I didn't know which way to go; I didn't stop to look at street signs. I just ran and ran. The wind stung my arm, but I didn't care. I just kept running. It almost felt like a dream where you are running but you aren't really getting anywhere. My legs felt almost weightless. Yet somehow, I kept running.

I don't know how, but I ended up near the high school I attended. I had a total of two friends in high school, a guy from gym and a girl who took piano with me. I introduced them to each other, and they started dating. We will call the girl Terry and the guy Matt. As I was running by the school, I saw them walking down the road together. I didn't really want them to see me, but before I could get out of their eyesight, I heard Terry call my name. So, I stopped running and made my way to them.

Of course, after the usual, "Hey, how are you?" Matt asked why my arm was wrapped up. Now, I could have made up a lie and just kept going, but before I realized what I was saying or doing, I was sobbing and telling them what had happened. They both just stood there looking at me in disbelief. Up until now, no one in the world knew what happened at my house behind closed doors.

Terry insisted that I go to her home and clean up until we could figure out what to do. I agreed, and so we all walked to her home. I begged them not to tell her parents for fear they would contact my stepmom or the police. I told her mom it was a skateboarding accident. She helped me clean it up and wrap it properly. She seemed concerned that I wasn't being truthful, but she never questioned me too deeply.

I couldn't stop thinking about leaving my sister behind. It was eating at me, and I just couldn't shake the feeling of wanting to check on her, so I called the house and tried disguising my voice. My stepmom answered, and I said I was one of my stepsister's friends and asked to speak to her. My stepmom immediately knew it was me—I guess I suck at voice impressions. It sounded like she began to cry. She begged me to tell her where I was and to come home.

I don't have any clue why, but it hurt me to hear her upset. I began thinking that maybe I was wrong for leaving. How was I going to survive on my own anyway? I could borrow some money and hitchhike to my grandmother's. That was a whole state away though. I cracked and gave in. I didn't want to involve my friends, so I told her I was at the high school.

She came and picked me up from the high school. There were no tears or signs of sadness when I got into the car, and not one word was spoken on the way to the house. When I got home, I saw Winnie out of the corner of my eye. Her eyes were red from crying, and her mouth was swollen and bleeding. I knew it was because of me and felt horrible. She had been beaten because she didn't know where I was. So many emotions ran through me in that moment. My stepmom told me to sit down because she wanted to talk. After a thorough interrogation and lots of empty promises of no more beatings, life was painless. But the beatings started again a week later.

This is what happens when the road looks hard and we don't think God will get us where we are going. Someone once said to me, "God wants to get you where He wants you more than you want to get where He wants you to be." Sometimes it's hard though. True, my home life was brutal, but to a fifteen-year-old me, being homeless and hitchhiking seemed a lot harder than taking a beating regularly.

So, I went right back into what God had given me a way out of. There are so many options I could have chosen instead of going back. Even when a situation is painful, it can be comforting to us because it is familiar. We know what to expect, and we don't have to have faith that things will or won't work out because we are comfortable where we are. There are no surprises, and we just condition ourselves to deal with what is familiar.

A battered wife will stay with her abuser because he has made her believe that even though her life is painful, there is no life and nothing better outside of what she currently has. It will be too hard for her to start over again. She believes that she can't do any better than where she is. These beliefs are all false!

Sis, you have a choice! It's not always easy, but it is always worth it in the end. You may have to work fast food for a few months or years while you find a career doing something you love. You may have to eat PB&J for a few months while you save money to get where you want to be. You may not be able to rock them designer clothes, bags, jewelry, or make-up that you did while you were a kept woman. But...

You will succeed. You will be happy. You will have a life outside of the pain. You will overcome the battles. You will be proud of the woman you are and the journey you took to become her! You will be able to look in the mirror and be happy with the woman you see looking back. Your scars won't be a reminder of the coming pain but symbols of a warrior who won the battle for her life.

Philippians 4:13 is one of the most quoted scriptures in the Bible. However, I believe we miss the word "all" in the passage. God didn't say some, a few, or most things. He said we can do *all* things in Christ Jesus. Do you believe that, sis? Or is it just a feel-good verse? Do you just quote it to lift others from their despair or because it is a popular verse?

Sis, believe it! Claim it! God doesn't say things He doesn't mean. He doesn't waste words. He meant it for you. The Bible says that we will do greater things than even Jesus did! John 14:12 declares,

"Very truly I tell you, whoever believes in Me will do the works I have been doing, and they will do even greater things than these, because I am going to the Father."

Did you catch that, sis? *Very truly.* Jesus said that. He wanted to make sure you heard Him and understood how serious He was. He wanted you to know the sincerity of this promise. Believe on it. Believe in Him and what He said. God wants more for you than you could ever imagine for yourself.

I know your situation looks tough. I know you don't see a better future for yourself. I know it's painful but familiar. I know you tell yourself that you don't have to be happy if you're comfortable. You were created for more, sis! Use God's eyes.

You are HER: **H**ighly favored. **E**mpowered. **R**edeemed. You are a queen because your Father is a King. And not just any king but The King. He put a purpose inside you so great that only you can achieve it. There is only one of you. He made you unique in every way and has given you authority to move mountains. You can overcome anything. It's there, I promise it is. I am living proof.

I opened that latch again at fifteen, but this time, my sister was with me. We made it to Georgia and never looked back. I have been on my own since then. It hasn't been easy. There were days I wanted to give up as I cried and went through pain. But God. He walked with me through it all. Here I am today, living proof that He is able and that through Him, I am able, speaking life and hope into women of all ages from the life that He gave me.

Sometimes the first step is hard. Sometimes you get overwhelmed because you want to see the entire outcome of the journey before you begin. Let me make it just a little bit easier for you, sis. Are you ready?

It only takes one step at a time, sis. Once you take the first step, just focus on the next. You don't have to see the end of the road; you just need to see the next step. God knows where you need to be, and He will get you there. He will be there to catch you every time you miss a step or can't find it.

Remember what we talked about? He will never leave you or forsake you. He will bring people into your life to lean on and pray for you and with you. You will be surrounded by angels to help you fight each battle. Yes, girl, sometimes it might be tough. It won't be a cake walk, but anything worth having is worth fighting for, right? So, let's fight, sis.

Let's get that armor (Eph. 6:10-18) on and get to work. Our little sisters are watching us. We must pave the way for them. We must be the ones to show them where we get our strength from. The world will lead them down a road of destruction. You know, sis; we've been there. Your path is set, and the journey is calling. All you have to do is take the first step. Are you ready?

Chapter Six

Pain. That word feels like a part of us sometimes, doesn't it? No matter what kind of pain we experience—mental, physical, spiritual, relational, or otherwise—it is like a growth that attaches itself to us. We try to mask it with different things— relationships, drugs, money, music, whatever gives us that few moments of reprieve.

When I was twenty-eight years old, I was told I had to have a complete hysterectomy due to prolapsed organs and endometriosis. Honestly, I wasn't upset about it. Sure, I was young and not ready for menopause, but I knew I wasn't having more children, so I was okay with it. No more monthly cycle sounded like a dream, if you know what I mean. What is the worst that could happen, right?

Well, sis, the doctor who performed the surgery was old enough to be my great-grandfather, and his mind was already fading, which was clear from the conversations we had. I thought my husband would fall over when the doctor asked me how the baby was doing when I went to my post-op appointment. After the nurse brought him back to reality, we just shook it off as a joke.

He was the doctor my insurance sent me to though, so again, I thought to myself *What's the worst that could happen?* Almost two months after my down time from the procedure, I started to have this excruciating pain in my right lower stomach. Now, I am not exaggerating, sis. This pain would hit me so suddenly and randomly, it would take my breath away. I can't count the times I was on the side of the road wondering if I was dying or in labor.

I went to the doctor and was told it was just scar tissue that it would go away in time. More times than I can count, I was looked at as a drug seeker. I was asked multiple times if I was suffering from depression and referred to a psychologist because it had to be something mental, I was told. Well, it didn't go away. It got worse, and each time I went back to see a doctor, I was told nothing was wrong and sent home. Each time was a harder blow than the last. I just couldn't understand. Who would *want* to feel this way?

After almost a full year of this routine, I started to think I was going crazy. I started to look for a psychiatrist to see if I was mentally unstable. No one could figure out what was wrong, so I must be making myself sick, right? I mean, I had to be loco if I was doing this to myself. Mental disorders ran in my family. Maybe I was starting to have the symptoms. I was at a loss. I didn't know what else to do.

During this time, I got new insurance and was referred to a different doctor. A friend asked me to see him before I went to see a psychiatrist. I had been to so many doctors that I was hesitant, but I agreed. For the first time, someone actually listened to me. He wanted the whole story, and I gave it to him. He asked if he could do an exploratory surgery to check out the area where I was having pain, and I said yes. Again, what was the worst that could happen?

I still remember waking up from that procedure and seeing my husband sitting next to me. The first thing I said was, "I'm crazy, aren't I?" He looked at me confused and asked if I had talked to the doctor. I told him I hadn't. He began to tell me that the doctor had found little pieces of metal, possibly surgical clips, in my body. He was able to remove them from my right side. I began to cry. I wasn't crazy. I wasn't mentally ill. I wasn't making myself sick. Then my husband dropped the bad news.

I had seven pieces on my left side, and they were only able to remove one. Because the pieces had been left in me for so long, they had grown into tissue and around nerves and tendons that were impossible to get to without damaging my quality of life. So, for the last ten years, I have dealt with pain spasms that I can't control with anything outside of pain medication. Sis, some days, I lay in a ball on my bed and just cry because there is nothing I can do. I refuse to live my life in a fog, so the only time I take pain medication is when I absolutely cannot handle the pain any longer.

I have prayed, had hands laid on me, and asked others to pray, yet I still have this pain. Once again, I would love to be able to tell you that I have just kept the faith and soldiered through, but I can't do that. I can't tell you a story of miraculous healing. I can't give you a feel-good quote about how God has miraculously taken the pain away from my life. I also can't tell you that I wish I could because then I wouldn't be able to tell you what I am about to tell you next.

I started to become bitter at one point. I was mad all the time. For months, I cried out and asked God why He wouldn't take this from me. I would sit in the shower for hours just crying and wondering if I just didn't have enough faith and that was why my prayers were going unanswered. Maybe that was why the laying of hands on my body didn't work. Wasn't it said we only need to have faith the size of a mustard seed? I had to have at least that, right?

Then one day it hit me like a piano falling from the seventeenth floor of a building. Healing does not always come in the form of God taking away the affliction. God doesn't always take our pains, troubles, or misery away. Instead, He gives us what we need to get through it. There are so many examples in the Bible of this. Most people think of Job, Jeremiah, or Paul when going through trials, and they are all great examples, but I look at Esther.

I absolutely love the story of Esther. I feel like I should have been born in an era when kings and queens were prominent. Esther was a young girl, barely a teenager. She was just fourteen, sis. Fourteen. Now, I don't know about you, but I was not thinking about marriage or anything to do with the subject at fourteen years old. I was still trying to figure out boys and why they smelled the way they do.

Esther was dragged away from her home and her family and then prepared to be a wife for a man she had never even met or spoken to. Can you imagine that wedding night? Now, sis, it was not like today where if you aren't ready, your husband understands and you get to wait until that time comes. One of the most important duties of a queen was to give the king sons. Henry VIII had multiple women executed for failure to do so. It was that big of a deal.

Sons were how kings left a legacy in the world. So, consummating the marriage was not taken lightly. As soon as the wedding was over, you were followed to a room where people stood around the marriage bed and watched as you consummated the marriage. There was no waiting, no talking, no pillow talk. No privacy or easing into it, just getting the deed done.

This young girl had to endure this—every awkward, embarrassing, painful moment. Could God have gotten her out of this situation or made it so she never was put in it from the start? Of course, He could have! I mean, we are talking about the same God Who parted the Red Sea for Moses.

However, remember what we talked about before? God's plan for our lives is so much bigger than just one moment. God knew Esther. He knew her heart and that it belonged to Him. He knew she was the one He would use to save His people from a horrible plot to wipe them out. He gave her what she needed to endure and fulfill her purpose, and He was with her through it all.

Every day I wake up, I pray for just one more day to get up and do what God wants me to do. Some days, it's hard, but I know that no matter what, if God has it for me, He will see me to it and through it. I know that He will give me the what I need to endure and fulfill my purpose, the purpose He gave to me. He wants greater for me greater than I want for myself. He is a good Father.

I know He could stop the pain completely if He wanted to, but true faith is when we make the choice to trust Him even when He doesn't give us what we want. Even in the garden of Gethsemane (Luke 22:42), Jesus had His moment when He asked God to take the cup from Him if He was willing. Then He followed with, "Not My Will, but Your will be done." God could have called Jesus to heaven right then and there, but that was not the plan, and so Jesus still trusted His Father and went to the cross.

I may deal with this pain for the rest of my life, but I will still do what God wants me to. I will have faith that He is good and will sustain me. I love what it says in 1 Peter 5:10,

"And the God of all grace, who called you to His eternal glory in Christ, after you have suffered a little while, will Himself restore you and make you strong, firm, and steadfast."

I don't know what a little while is, but I will hold to the promise of restoration because I know that our God is a God who doesn't break His promises. I know restoration is coming in this life or the next, and in the words of one of my favorite Christian hip hop artists Trip Lee, until then, I'll be praising in the waiting room.

Chapter Seven

Do you remember your first kiss? First love? I sure do. When I was fifteen, I was living in Georgia with my aunt and uncle, and I met a boy who used to come and work for my uncle from time to time. He was a little older than me and looked much more like a young man than a teenage boy. We began dating, and one night in the backseat of my uncle's car, he kissed me good night. Now, we aren't talking deep make-out kissing—just a simple kiss on the lips. I was expecting it to be like fireworks on the Fourth of July, but it was just a simple thing that happened.

That relationship didn't last long at all. Then I started dating a boy I went to school with who was the first cousin of my best friend at the time. It was the most serious relationship I had ever been in up until this point. He was older, so he introduced me to things like making out early in the relationship.

I was a little star-struck with him. He wrote me poems and love songs all the time, and he was old enough to drive, so of course he was one of the cooler kids in school. Since we were dating, I got to hang out with the older kids, which was different for me. I felt important.

On the last day of school, we were watching movies in our last class of the day. I was an advanced student, so we had a class together. It was one of my favorite classes. I really liked school, and I made good grades and received honors in a few of my classes.

I was wearing some super cute overall shorts over a tank top. It was the last day of school, so we got a little bit of freedom with the dress code. You know how there are those clothes that just make you feel super cute. This was one of those outfits. He sat behind me and began with what most people call roaming hands.

I was uncomfortable. I didn't want him to touch me the way he was, but I didn't say anything because I didn't want him to be mad at me. I didn't want to break up, but I didn't want what was going on either. When I got home, I took the longest shower of my life and cried for what seemed like hours. Then I got up the nerve to call him. I told him how I felt, and he broke up with me a few minutes later. I was upset because I thought what we had meant more than that, but as young love goes, I quickly got over it.

When I turned sixteen, I moved in with my aunt and her son, who was my best friend growing up. He was adopted, but I didn't know that until much later in life. We started school together, and it was the first time I had a home that I was happy in. We did everything together—school, work, and even church. I started to feel different about him at some point, like an attraction that hadn't been there before. It was like a feeling we both had that we just didn't talk about.

I am a better writer than speaker, so I wrote him a letter. One night, he came into my room and told me that he knew and that he felt the same. He was dating someone from school at the time though, so it just kind of went unaddressed after that. I was okay with it. I mean, he had been dating this girl for a while, and we were known as cousins around school. How weird would that be for us to start a relationship? Life just went on as it had for the last four months.

One morning, I woke up to a weight on top of me. I opened my eyes to see my cousin naked and taking off my pajama bottoms. Shock doesn't even begin to describe what I felt in that moment. I almost thought I was having a nightmare. This was too real though. I just couldn't process what was happening.

I didn't scream. I didn't yell for help. I didn't push him away from me. I simply looked at him and said stop. It was like he didn't hear me. He just kept going. He didn't hold me down. He didn't yell, hit me, or cover my mouth. He just went through the motions. All I could do is lay there. I stared at the ceiling until it was over.

When he was finished, he got up, ran his fingers across my face, and left the room. I don't know how long I laid there. I don't know when the tears started or stopped. It was like a dream I couldn't wake up from. I just couldn't understand how this person who I trusted, loved, and admired could do this to me. How could he take something he knew was precious to me? Why wouldn't he listen to me when I said stop? Was this rape?

It couldn't be. He didn't hit me. He didn't hold me down. He wasn't violent. Rape is all those things, isn't it? When you see it on television or hear people talking about it, that is what it looks like, right? Rape is a violent act, not a subtle one. Isn't it?

Sis, let me be the first to tell you if you don't know already. No means no! I don't care if you shout it from the top of your lungs or whisper it low enough for the ants to hear. No one has the right to take away your choice to consent. He knew

I didn't want to. He knew that I held my virginity in high regard. It was something we had talked about. My whole life, my choices had been taken away from me.

My virginity was the one thing I had left that I was holding onto until I was married. I had told him about my previous experience with the uncomfortable touching. He knew, and yet even when I said stop, he kept going. Maybe if I had screamed or tried to fight him off, I would have been successful. Sis, sometimes you can't. Our bodies are mysterious in that way. Sometimes they freeze up and we can't do anything but just breathe. Sometimes that is how we survive.

Never be ashamed of how you survive. The only One who sits in a place to judge you is God. He is the only One you must answer to for anything you have ever done. For years, I beat myself up because I felt I should have handled the situation differently and maybe I would have been able to save my virtue. You know what, sis? It's not my fault. It's his. He took advantage of me. He made a choice to ignore my words and tears. He took my virtue away from me.

There is no excuse in the world for what he did. Let me tell you about a real man. When I met my husband and I decided that I wanted to be intimate, he must have asked me ten times before we actually did anything to make sure I was sure. He asked if I was ready. He never once forced or tried to coerce me into something I didn't want to do. No matter how far we got, he kept asking. Was I okay, was I sure, did I want to stop at any time. That is a man, sis, someone who makes sure you are okay with what is happening; someone who respects your boundaries even when emotions and hormones are raging.

I don't care if it is a first date or you've been married for twenty years. Never let anyone tell you that you don't have a choice. Never let anyone make you think that that if the act isn't violent or painful, then it is okay. Your no is your no, and it doesn't matter how loud it is. Body language is a thing, and men can read it just like we can. Don't let them tell you different. If he can tell when you want him, he can tell when you don't, sis.

That boy took a piece of me that I can never get back. It took me twenty years to come to terms with that, and it took me longer to forgive myself for not reacting the way I thought I should have. Thank God I have a husband who will just hold me on the nights when the nightmares haunt me, a man who will stop and just listen to me when the flashbacks come and I can't deal. I am not fully healed yet, and it has been over twenty years, but I can say that I am healing. I can say that I don't blame myself anymore. I can say that I don't let that boy and what he did to me control my life anymore. I can say that I am not a victim; I am a survivor.

Chapter Eight

"You're a grandmother?" I hear this at least once a week. Yes, I am a grandmother. Yes, my son is sixteen. Alright, sis, buckle up because this chapter is going to get rocky. As a mom, I have made some mistakes. Okay, I admit I have made lots of mistakes. I have fed my kids cake for breakfast and cereal for dinner. They didn't learn sign language when they were babies, and they drank soda from a sippy cup. Yeah, I'm that mom.

Now for my moms who got it together and you know what college your kid is going to attend and you haven't even had them yet, I salute you. I am not that mom. I am the definition of a hot mess express. My hair stays in a messy bun, and caffeine stays in my hand. My kids are my life, though, and I wouldn't trade it for anything in the world.

I had my oldest son in my early twenties. When I tell you that that kid was my greatest joy, blessing, and accomplishment at that age, I am not exaggerating. As mentioned earlier, all I ever wanted was to be a mom, and when I had my son, it was like God heard my heart and answered me with The Boy. Yes, that is what I call him. He is a Jr. named after his daddy and rightly so.

He is like him in every way possible. When he was little, he was a mama's boy, though, through and through. There was no one else in this world who held a place higher in his life than me. Even as he got older and started school, he would still hug me and tell me he loved me before leaving the car to go into school. He went through a rough patch when the affair happened, but we got through it together. Then he started high school.

High school was a bittersweet thing for me. I couldn't wait to see what kind of young man he would become. I was excited for things like football, prom, and graduation, all the things parents look forward to when their kids start high school. You start to see in your mind what your child's future is going to look like. What I was not ready for was The Girl.

After only about a month into freshman year, The Boy met The Girl in ROTC, and they began dating. She was a pretty girl with long blonde hair and blue eyes. She was funny and made him laugh, and they seemed to have a lot in common. Things were good at first until suddenly they weren't.

We started to get to know her family background, and it was not good. Her mom was strung out on drugs and had boyfriends in and out of the house regularly. They lived in a run-down trailer that looked like something out of a *Hoarders* episode. The first time I met her mom, I lost my breath when she came out of the house from the smell that followed her. She was clearly intoxicated. I immediately did not like the situation for my son. This was not the type of family I saw him marrying into.

Over the next few months, The Girl would come over and hang out with my son, but I would not allow him to go anywhere with her or her family. Then Hurricane Matthew hit. The Boy called me and asked if his girlfriend could come stay with us during the hurricane because her mom had left her home alone while they took shelter at her grandmother's. I could not believe this. There is no way a mother would leave her fourteen-year-old daughter to fend for herself during a category 4 storm.

I drove to the trailer park to find out what was going on. I found her there alone, so I took her home with me. I couldn't believe it, but it was true. Her mother had just abandoned her. I tried calling social services, but I was told they already had a case open on her and there was nothing else that could be done. So, she stayed with us until her mother came home. Now, I know what you're thinking. No wonder she is a grandmother—she moved the girlfriend in! Sis, I'm not that crazy. My son had a sleeping area in my room with the door deadbolted and an extra-large dog crate pushed in front of the door. There was no recess at my house, if you know what I mean.

After they had been dating for four months, I woke up one night, and my son was gone. Now, I was not even in the ballpark of thinking he had run away. I was thinking someone had kidnapped him or worse. My son loves to run, and he would go running all the time, so I called him to see if that was where he was. No answer. Then I saw his headphones on the table. There was no way he went running without his headphones; it just wouldn't happen. So, I called him again. Nothing.

My husband was out of town with my youngest son at a church retreat. I called him, and at this point, I was clearly panicking. I got in my car and started driving, looking up and down the road for my son, thinking the worst. My husband told me to call the police, so I did, and they told me to go home and wait. I called my sister Winnie, and she came over with her entire family to help me look for The Boy. I called everyone I knew, including his friend and The Girl.

The Girl told me she hadn't seen or talked to him. Hours went by, and nothing. I called her again and begged her, saying he wasn't in trouble but to please just let me know he was okay. She then began to tell me that he was on his way to her house but never made it. I literally hit my knees in the driveway. Not only had he run away, but now he could be hurt somewhere, and no one knew where he was. Every piece inside my heart broke at that moment.

About two minutes later, a cop car pulled up. An officer got out and walked up to me, asking if I was the one who reported a missing child. I tried to catch my breath and explain to her what he looked like. She held her hand out to stop me from talking and told me she had my son in the back of her car, and his bike was in her trunk. If you think your heart can't break any more after the initial break, let me tell you, mine did. My son had run away, and I was devastated.

My son knew about my anxiety. How could he do this to me? How could he hurt me this way? All

I could do was cry. I was so angry but hurt at the same time. Winne called my husband to let him know we had found The Boy. The police officer had seen him riding his bike and stopped him when she heard the call over the scanner about a missing boy. He had been on his way to see The Girl.

The next day, I sat him down in front of me and found out that they were having sex. Talk about kicking a mom while she's down! Not only was he running away, he was skipping school and having sex. He was fourteen! I pulled him out of school and started homeschooling him the very next week. Things were better for about two months. He got really involved in church and made new friends. I thought he was over The Girl, so I let him go back to public school his sophomore year.

The next summer, he came home from church and told us she was pregnant. I couldn't believe it. He was fifteen. How could she be pregnant? How could this happen? He had been doing so well. He was writing music and volunteering with the youth at church. By all outward appearances, he was done with her and had moved on. What had I missed? This couldn't possibly be happening to my family.

That year was the last year that my husband and I volunteered at church youth camp. That was also the year that we got some of the best advice during this period in our lives, and it came from a high school senior studying to be a pastor. We blamed ourselves for the pregnancy. We weren't strict enough. We didn't pay enough attention. We had to have done something wrong for this to happen. Here is what this brilliant young man said.

God is our Father, and He is perfect. He doesn't make mistakes. He created Adam and Eve and gave them everything they could ever possibly want or need. Even in all His perfection, Adam and Eve still sinned. Was this God's fault? No. God made each of us and gave us free will. It is that free will that allows us to make our own choices, including my son.

Sis, we can give our children the best life they could ever possibly want, and they can still turn away and become people who we don't know. It is hard, and a battle that some of us fight every single day. The beauty of my story is that The Girl now has a family that will never cast her out, and we have a beautiful granddaughter that God gave us during all the chaos. Not all stories have happy endings though. I know a few mamas who have had sad endings to their stories of struggle. I know they blame themselves at times.

Mama, I'm talking to you. The choices that your children make are not your fault. You can only give them the best you possibly can and then let them do with it what they will. They have their own personalities, views, and free will. We can only lead them in the right direction; it is their choice whether to follow or not. It's hard, mama, I know it is. At times, I look at my son's life now and imagine how it could have been different.

If your kid is an addict, alcoholic, promiscuous, in jail, or has nothing to do with you, that is not your fault mama. Our children must find their own way at a certain point, and sometimes, as much as we want to, we are not privy to everything they go through in life. They are not always open with us, so sometimes they find other ways to deal. Sometimes peer pressure wins. That is not your fault. All you can do is be the very best mom to the best of your abilities that God gave you and pray every single day for them babies.

My pastor says you do all you can possibly do and then get out of the way and let God do what only He can do. Mama, you have got to let go of the blame. You have got to drop that self-doubt. Surround yourself with other mamas who can be supportive. The phrase it takes a village isn't just cute talk; it really does. I am so grateful for my little village. They walked with my family through some tough times.

Now, don't hear what I'm not saying. I love my granddaughter, and I firmly believe that God has a purpose for every single life He brings into this world. That doesn't mean that I can't imagine sometimes what my son's life would look like if he wasn't a father at sixteen. It could have been worse, and it could have been better. I don't think I will ever know this side of heaven. I don't need to though.

All I know is that I hold tightly to the promise of God in Romans 8:28, which says,

"And we know that in all things God works for the good of those who love Him, who have been called according to His purpose."

This verse is something I constantly repeat to myself because if I don't, the devil will have me thinking that I am being punished, that God doesn't love me, or that He's mad at me. This is not true. Sis, the devil is a liar, and the biggest lie that he can make you believe is that God is not for you. Don't believe it, sis. Don't you give him that satisfaction. Your Father loves you, adores you, and is always on your side.

Sometimes life is out of our control; most of the time it is. So, we put our hope and trust in the One who holds all control. People are out of our control, but we can pray for them and lift them up to God. We may not always see the fruit of our prayers, but they are there. Remember, sis—God is for you, and He is working everything together for good. Even when we can't see it, we can hold fast and know that our God is not One who breaks His promises.

Chapter Nine

I still remember the sinking feeling I got when I found out I was pregnant with my youngest son. My oldest son had just turned seven months, and the doctor told me that I was three months along. I was in complete shock and disbelief. How could I be pregnant again and three months along? If you remember the previous story about my first two pregnancies, you know why I was so shocked.

Well, nine months later, my youngest son was born—healthy, happy, and hyperactive. He never stopped moving, not even when he slept. He was up every two hours like clockwork for a bottle. Let me just tell you, sis—this mama was not ready for baby number two when he came. He was completely unplanned.

As my son got older, we realized that he was different from other kids, not in a completely obvious way but just certain things he would do and say. He was a talker and loved to video himself doing everything. To this day, he loves to watch himself on camera, and theater is his favorite class in school. He loves to act and is such an awesome performer.

When he was in first grade, he was diagnosed with ADHD. I am one of those parents who thinks that this specific condition is extremely over-diagnosed in our time, but as my son got older, I watched him struggle more and more with it. I battled with myself about putting him on medication. I didn't want to do it, but I hated seeing him struggle with basic things like remembering to brush his teeth.

We did research and reluctantly ended up putting him on a medication for the condition. He was not himself. He was withdrawn, silent, sad, and a recluse. This was so out of character for him. My son brings joy, smiles, and laughter to every environment he is in. It is just who he is. He loves Jesus and is so passionate about ministering to the younger generation. He lost all of that when we medicated him. He began passing all his classes and getting straight A's, but he just wasn't himself.

I was beside myself. What was the best choice for him? Should I have taken a different route? Was I a bad mother for medicating my child? Sis, let me tell you, life throws us things every day that we didn't expect, from sickness or a traffic jam to a diagnosis that your child has special needs.

I watched my niece grow up with Asperger's, and it was something that made me admire the type of mom my sister was. Why was it so hard for me to accept that my son had special needs as well? It just didn't look the same as someone else's.

Let me tell you, sis, I have watched and spent time with so many children who have special needs, and they see the world completely differently than you and me. I always say special needs because the word disabled seems so invalidating to me. Honestly, I think all people are special needs. We are all human and need different things to adjust to this thing called life. We all have special needs that we need met to be functional human beings.

To me, my son was always just different— not more or less, just different. I now see that we label things like ADHD, Asperger's, OCD, etc. disabilities because in the human eye, we don't understand them. They don't fit into this box of normal that we have made. But what is actually normal?

I think these things are just special abilities given to us. People with ADHD may forget things and be messy and super hyper, but they are also super intelligent, passionate, driven, and some of the greatest minds we have ever seen.

My son has a relationship with God at such a young age that I admire and sometimes envy. I know, I know, envy is a sin. I'm human, sis! It is so amazing to hear him talk about things that God has shown him, his love for the ministry, and his relationship with Jesus.

Today he is on the youth worship team and teaches during services. The kids absolutely love him. He loves on them and talks to them like little people, not babies, and teaches them how much Jesus loves them. He plays with them and gets on their level. Some would call him immature and other things. I think God gave him a purpose, and he is diving into it.

Maybe you have one of these special needs or maybe you're a mama like me with a child who has a special need. Don't focus on the label, sis. It is the world's label, not God's. God called you chosen for a reason, and no matter what purpose you were chosen for, He has equipped you with everything you need to fill that purpose.

Same thing goes for your babies. God doesn't make mistakes. I truly believe there is a purpose in this world for every single person. We don't always know what the purpose is, but we know that God doesn't do anything without one, and that includes breathing life into each of us.

My son was not planned, but he brings more joy into this world and our lives than I could have ever imagined. I can't even imagine what I would do without his quirky little smile or his constant laugh echoing through my home. We didn't plan on having a child with special needs, but they make him who he is. He may have a special need, but he is perfect in every way because he is perfectly made by the One who makes no mistakes.

So are you, sis. No matter what position you find yourself in, God has you there for a reason. Trust Him and walk in your purpose. He won't let you fall. Don't let the world tell you that you can't or shouldn't because you don't think like everyone else does. Get into God's Word and see what God says about you. These needs didn't just arise in the last decade or so. I have no doubt that some of the people from the Bible probably had similar needs.

No matter what the world tells you, it is not wrong to need things or understand things differently than others. It is not wrong for you to not want the same things that this world says you need to be successful. There is no shame in feeling things, having emotions, or communicating differently than someone else does or in the way they think you should.

God uses people where they are and for the purpose they were chosen for. He made us all different and unique in our own ways. This includes the way we see, feel, and communicate. It's not a mistake, and it's not a disability.

No matter what labels the world comes up with from now until Jesus calls us home—and trust me, sis, I have a feeling there will be many—the only labels you need to focus on are child of God, fearfully and wonderfully made, and made in the image of God. The rest are irrelevant.

Chapter Ten

You ever stand in front of your mirror and wonder who that person is staring back at you? I mean, like really sit there and think about who that person is? Maybe you look at the wrinkles starting to form on your face or spot a grey hair coming in. I find myself wondering what happened to the thirty-plus years I have been in this world, how I got to be where I am so soon, who I am today compared to who I was yesterday, last month, ten years ago.

Most of us look in the mirror and think we need to skip that dessert after dinner the next few nights. Some think about ordering weight loss products or age-defying creams or signing up for a get-rich-quick seminar. Sis, can I just tell you that I have done all of the above. It's time for a change.

My identity is not found in the size of my clothes, the money in my account, how many books I write, or the amount of people who are going to show up when I die. My identity is found in Christ. For more than ten years, I bought every weight loss product you can think of. I spent well over $7,000 on weight loss products and ended up the hospital three times from bad reactions. It was not a successful three years.

I finally found one that worked for me and lost over sixty pounds. Don't get too excited or happy for me yet. This company was a multi-level marketing company, so of course when I got these results, they wanted me to start marketing and selling the product. They sold me the whole American dream, a life of luxury and wealth and time with my family. I didn't just jump in; I dove headfirst and hit the bottom of the pool.

Let's put it this way, sis—I put so much money into this company and this "dream" that my family was homeless for almost two months. Yeah, it was that serious. Now, let me just say that it wasn't all bad. I met a lot of people who are now my family today. Yes, I am that person where blood doesn't mean jack to me when it comes to family. Family is so much deeper and complex than just DNA. But that is a story for another day.

After a few months, we finally got back on our feet, but I had to do a lot of soul searching during this time. Why did I let my family go through that? It was so when people looked at me, they wouldn't see an overweight, jobless, stay-at-home mom. That was what I saw when I looked in the mirror, so that had to be what everyone else saw too, right? Was I really that shallow?

Yes, sis, yes I was. I am not proud of it. Is it really shallow though to feel the way we do about other people's opinions? Don't we have validation in the way we feel because some girls in high school told us we were less than? Now to add to my list of faults I am shallow too? I felt the stares every time I walked out the door. I heard the whispers every time I would pass a group of people. Sis, can I just tell you that so much of that is in our heads.

Don't get me wrong; there is and will always be people who are going to talk about you, look down at you, and gossip. Always. There will always be girls who think that to validate themselves they must invalidate someone else. It is just the way of things. It doesn't have to be though. We can start now and change it by setting the example of validating our sisters in love, kindness, acceptance, and inclusion. Everyone we meet isn't a "mean girl," and we need stop projecting that thought process onto everyone we encounter.

The God of all things, Master and Creator of the entire universe created you. He knew who you would be and become before you ever even had an idea of who you are. I know I said this earlier, but I really need you to get this, sis. We are women. When God created Eve, He didn't create her the way He did everything else. The beginning of Genesis 2:19 says,

"Now the Lord God had formed out of the ground all the wild animals and all the birds in the sky."

From the ground, all these things were formed. Have you ever taken just a moment to look and appreciate nature and the beauty that it holds? I love nature. It makes me feel close to God and loved by Him because He gave it to man as a gift (Gen. 2:19b). There is so much beauty in nature, and yet it all came from the ground. Not you though, sis. Genesis 2:23 says,

"Then the Lord God made a woman from the rib he had taken out of the man, and he brought her to the man."

Remember in the first chapter of Genesis, it says that God made man in *His* image (Gen. 1:26). So, when God made you, He knew that you had to be special, more special than nature, animals, and elements. So, He pulled a piece from the man He had made in His image and made you. Not the ground, the sea, or the sky—you are made in the image of the Father, and that means that you are flawless, sis.

Flawless. You can look in that mirror a hundred times a day, and this will remain true.

Now God also says that our bodies are His temple. In 1 Corinthians 6:19, the Word says,

"Do you not know that your body is a temple of the Holy Spirit within you, whom you have from God? You are not your own."

So, if our bodies are the temple of God, we should take care of them. Now, I don't know about you, but I am not a house cleaning person. I hate cleaning house with a passion. It is just not something I like. So, from time to time, my house gets out of order, if you will. It is no different with my body. I let my body get out of order sometimes. I don't watch what I put in it, so it gets out of control.

Now, sis, when I say what I put in it, I am not just talking about food. This is so much deeper than that. I don't always watch what I put in my ears, in front of my eyes, or the environment I place myself in. These things are important, sis. Once again, one of my favorite hip hop artists has a song that says,

"Your mind is a powerful place and what you feed it can affect you in a powerful way."

If we are consistently putting garbage in, then garbage will eventually be what starts to seep out. This is so much deeper than outside beauty. Let me explain it this way.

I have a friend. We met her and her husband at a Bible study a few years ago. One night, my husband and I were talking about people we know. He asked me who I thought the most beautiful person I knew was, and I immediately said her name. He smiled and said he thought the same. Now, this woman is not a model. Even though she is beautiful physically, she is not a celebrity or even a pillar of the community, per se.

However, she is without a doubt the most beautiful woman I have ever met in my life. She is sweet to every single person she meets, and there is not one person who knows her who won't tell you the same thing. Even while watching her go through one of the hardest times in her life when losing her son, I saw this woman smile through the pain and continue to give of herself. She volunteers with the women's prison ministry and helps anyone and everyone she meets in need. She always has a kind word and can be the biggest cheerleader in your circle. She is gorgeous and not because of the brand of makeup she wears, the size of her clothes, or the neighborhood she lives in.

She is beautiful because the light of Christ illuminates her and her life, and we can see that in the way she carries herself and lives. There is nothing in this world more beautiful than the love our Father has for us. He demonstrated that in Christ. If Christ lives in us, people should be able to see that, and it makes you beautiful. That is where your identity is, sis—in the love of Christ. You are God's daughter, and He gave up His Son so that He could have a relationship with you.

What do we do when things get out of order? We put them back.

If you feel out of order, then do something about it. My pastor says that if you spend time worrying about something you can change, it's pointless, and if you spend time worrying about something you can't change, it's also pointless.

If you can change something, then do it. If you can't change it, then leave it alone. Now, not being *able* to change something and making excuses are two different things. We must be honest with ourselves and know when we are just making excuses. But, sis, let's not complain and gaslight ourselves to believe we can't change something that we know with some effort we can.

Sis, *please,* if you don't get anything else from this chapter, get this.

You are fearfully and wonderfully made

The Daughter of The King

Chosen by God for God

Don't ever let *anyone*—not the parents who birthed you, the people who share your genetic code, your best friend from down the street since elementary school, the man who sleeps next to you, the children you brought into this world, or the woman in the grocery store who is looking at your sundress and Crocs like a serious fashion injustice—make you feel less than the beautiful, inspiring, strong, amazing woman who you are.

You *are* H.E.R.
Highly Favored
Empowered
Redeemed

Don't hide her any longer. Rock that tangled mess of hair, eat watermelon in your oatmeal, talk loudly, be spontaneously kind, and let people continue to say, "It's her." This is who God created you to be. He has called you, empowered you, redeemed you, and given you purpose. So, it's time, sis. Are you ready?

Find her. Accept her. Be her. Love her.

CPSIA information can be obtained
at www.ICGtesting.com
Printed in the USA
BVHW031947310821
615711BV00007B/175